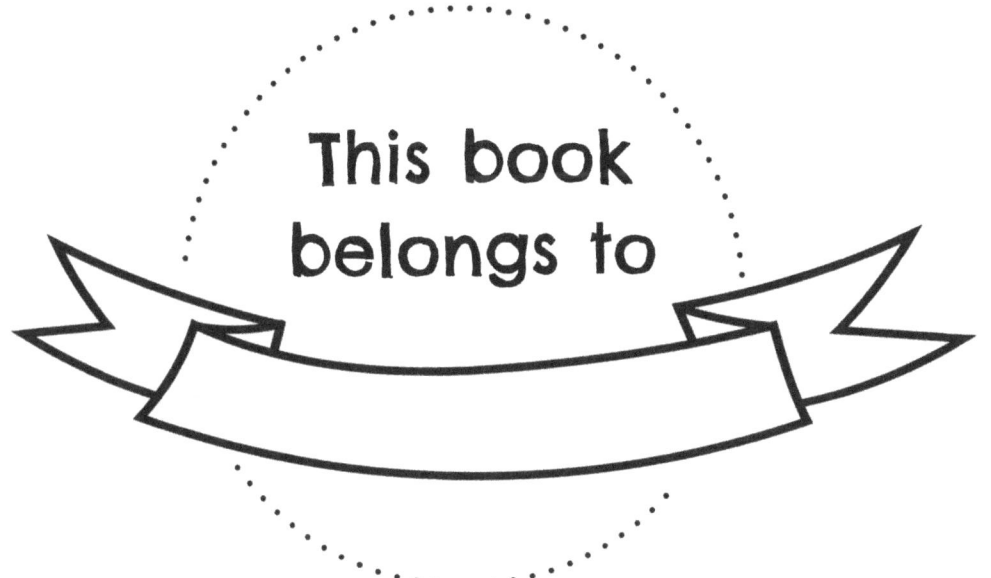

100 Bible Memory Verses: Every Kid Should Know by Heart

Copyright © 2024 Olivet Publishing Pty Ltd
All rights reserved.
Published by Olivet Publishing, an imprint of Olivet Publishing Pty Ltd. No part of this publication may be reproduced, stored in a retrieval system, or transmitted in any form or by any means—electronic, mechanical, photocopying, recording, or otherwise—without prior written permission from the publisher, except for brief quotations used in reviews, educational settings, or permitted uses under applicable copyright law.

ISBNs:
Paperback: 978-1-7644101-1-3

Scripture Credits:
Scripture quotations taken from the NASB® (New American Standard Bible®). Copyright © 1960, 1971, 1977, 1995, 2020 by The Lockman Foundation. Used by permission. All rights reserved. www.lockman.org
Scripture quotations marked (CEV) are taken from the Contemporary English Version. Copyright © 1991, 1992, 1995 by American Bible Society. Used by permission.
Scripture quotations are from The ESV® Bible (The Holy Bible, English Standard Version®). Copyright © 2001 by Crossway, a publishing ministry of Good News Publishers. Used by permission. All rights reserved.
Scripture quotations marked (NIV) are taken from the Holy Bible, New International Version® (NIV®). Copyright © 1973, 1978, 1984, 2011 by Biblica, Inc.™
Used by permission of Zondervan. All rights reserved worldwide. www.zondervan.com
"NIV" and "New International Version" are trademarks registered in the U.S. Patent & Trademark Office by Biblica, Inc.™
Scripture taken from the New King James Version® (NKJV®). Copyright © 1982 by Thomas Nelson. Used by permission. All rights reserved.
Scripture quotations taken from the Holy Bible, New Living Translation (NLT). Copyright © 1996, 2004, 2015 by Tyndale House Foundation. Used by permission of Tyndale House Publishers, Inc., Carol Stream, Illinois 60188. All rights reserved.

Edited and produced by Olivet Publishing Pty Ltd.
First Olivet Publishing Edition, 2024.

Introduction

Welcome to the start of an exciting, and life-changing journey!

This book is more than just a collection of Bible verses; it's an invitation to store God's word deep within you. As you memorize these verses, you're doing something incredibly important and powerful—you're inscribing God's word on your heart.

As you set out on this scripture memory adventure, know that YOU have what it takes to train your brain to remember the word of God. If it seems challenging at first, remember that with a little practice and determination, and the help of the Lord, you'll be amazed at how much you can remember (and never forget).

If you ever find yourself in a place where you don't have your Bible with you—maybe you're at school, playing with friends, or even facing a tough day. When you've committed scripture to memory, you have a treasure chest of God's words right inside you. These words can guide you, comfort you, and remind you of God's love and promises, no matter where you are.

As you start this journey, remember that the word of God is living and active (Hebrews 4:12). It's not just words on a page; it's alive! And when God's word lives in you, it can have a great impact on your life. You'll find that you can bring scripture into your conversations with friends and family, share God's truth, and be a light to others.

2 Timothy 3:15 reminds us, "...from childhood you have been acquainted with the sacred writings, which are able to make you wise for salvation through faith in Christ Jesus." As you grow, these scriptures will be like seeds planted in your heart, growing wisdom, strength, and a deep connection to God.

And remember, just like Jesus said in Matthew 4:4, "'Man shall not live by bread alone, but by every word that comes from the mouth of God.'" These verses are your spiritual food, nourishing your spirit and helping you grow strong in your faith.

So, get ready to fill your heart with God's word. You're about to begin an amazing adventure—one that will bless you for the rest of your life!

Bible Abbreviations

NASB: New American Standard Bible

CEV: Contemporary English Version

ESV: English Standard Version

NIV: New International Version

WEB: World English Bible

KJV: King James Version

NKJV: New King James Version

ASV: American Standard Version

NLT: New Living Translation

Memory Verse #1

For God so loved the world that he gave his one and only Son, that whoever believes in him shall not perish but have eternal life.

JOHN 3:16 (NIV)

Memory Verse #2

If you openly declare that Jesus is Lord and believe in your heart that God raised him from the dead, you will be saved.

ROMANS 10:9 (NLT)

If you would like to accept Jesus as your Lord and Savior, turn to page 104 and there is a special prayer you can pray to be saved!

Memory Verse #3

He Himself brought our sins in His body up on the cross, so that we might die to sin and live for righteousness; by His wounds you were healed.

1 PETER 2:24 (NASB)

Memory Verse #4

I am writing to you, little children, because your sins are forgiven for his name's sake.

1 JOHN 2:12 (ESV)

Memory Verse #5

The Lord is my shepherd, I will not be in need. He lets me lie down in green pastures; He leads me beside quiet waters. He restores my soul; He guides me in the paths of righteousness for the sake of His name.

PSALM 23:1-4 (NASB)

Question:
Has there been a time in your life when Jesus, like a Good Shepherd, has guided you along the right path?

Memory Verse #6

By this everyone will know that you are my disciples, if you love one another.

JOHN 13:35 (NIV)

Memory Verse #7

If I speak in the tongues of men and of angels, but have not love, I am a noisy gong or a clanging cymbal.

1 CORINTHIANS 13:1 (ESV)

Memory Verse #8

Don't let anyone think less of you because you are young. Be an example to all believers in what you say, in the way you live, in your love, your faith, and your purity.

1 TIMOTHY 4:12 (NLT)

Memory Verse #9

Love is patient and kind. Love is not jealous or boastful or proud or rude. It does not demand its own way. It is not irritable, and it keeps no record of being wronged. It does not rejoice about injustice but rejoices whenever the truth wins out.

1 CORINTHIANS 13:4-6 (NLT)

Prayer of the day:

Lord God, help me to love those around me today with a 1 Corinthians 13 kind of love.

Memory Verse #10

Love the Lord your God with all your heart and with all your soul and with all your mind and with all your strength.

MARK 12:30 (NIV)

Did you know? The very first commandment that God gave us was to love the Lord our God with all our heart, soul and mind.

Memory Verse #11

Your word is a lamp to my feet And a light to my path.

PSALM 119:105 (NASB)

Memory Verse #12

Whoever dwells in the shelter of the Most High will rest in the shadow of the Almighty.

PSALM 91:1 (NIV)

Memory Verse #13

For He will give His angels orders concerning you, To protect you in all your ways.

PSALM 91:11 (NASB)

Memory Verse #14

"For I know the plans I have for you," declares the Lord, "plans to prosper you and not to harm you, plans to give you hope and a future."

JEREMIAH 29:11 (NIV)

Say this out loud: God has a plan for my life, and in him I have a HOPE and a FUTURE.

Memory Verse #15

In nothing be anxious; but in everything by prayer and supplication with thanksgiving let your requests be made known unto God.

PHILIPPIANS 4:6-7 (ASV)

Memory Verse #16

Rejoice always; pray without ceasing.

1 THESSALONIANS 5:16-17 (ASV)

Memory Verse #17

Our Father in heaven,
hallowed be your name.
Your kingdom come,
your will be done,
on earth as it is in heaven.
Give us this day our daily bread,
and forgive us our debts,
as we also have forgiven our debtors.
And lead us not into temptation,
but deliver us from evil.

MATTHEW 6:9-13 (ESV)

PS: This scripture is also known as The Lord's Prayer. When you're done memorizing it, why not try and pray it out loud every day?

Memory Verse #18

For the eyes of the Lord are on the righteous and his ears are attentive to their prayer, but the face of the Lord is against those who do evil.

1 PETER 3:12 (NIV)

Remember:
The Lord is always listening to your prayers, no matter how quietly you pray them.

Memory Verse #19

Children, obey your parents in the Lord: for this is right.

EPHESIANS 6:1 (ASV)

Memory Verse #20

We can make our plans, but the LORD determines our steps.

PROVERBS 16:9 (NLT)

Memory Verse #21

for you created my inmost being; you knit me together in my mother's womb. I praise you because I am fearfully and wonderfully made; your works are wonderful, I know that full well.

PSALM 139:13-14 (NIV)

Reminder:
YOU have been made by the hands of God. YOU are special. YOU are unique.

Memory Verse #22

But he answered, "It is written, "'Man shall not live by bread alone, but by every word that comes from the mouth of God.'"

MATTHEW 4:4 (ESV)

Question: What do you think it means to 'not live by bread alone' as Jesus said?

Memory Verse #23

Fear of the LORD is the foundation of wisdom. Knowledge of the Holy One results in good judgment.

PROVERBS 9:10 (NLT)

Memory Verse #24

Now faith is assurance of things hoped for, proof of things not seen.

HEBREWS 11:1 (WEB)

Memory Verse #25

And we know that to them that love God all things work together for good, even to them that are called according to his purpose.

ROMANS 8:28 (ASV)

Question:
Can you think of a time in your life when God turned a not-so-great situation into something for your good?

Memory Verse #26

Store your treasures in heaven, where moths and rust cannot destroy, and thieves do not break in and steal.

MATTHEW 6:20 (NLT)

Question: How do you think you can store up for yourself treasures in heaven?

Memory Verse #27

Whoever is generous to the poor lends to the LORD, and he will repay him for his deed.

PROVERBS 19:17 (ESV)

Memory Verse #28

What then shall we say to these things? If God is for us, who can be against us?

ROMANS 8:31 (NKJV)

Memory Verse #29

Therefore I say to you, do not worry about your life, what you will eat or what you will drink; nor about your body, what you will put on. Is not life more than food and the body more than clothing?

MATTHEW 6:25 (NKJV)

Question:

Have you ever worried about something, only to have God show you that you really had nothing to fear?

Memory Verse #30

Ask and it will be given to you; seek and you will find; knock and the door will be opened to you.

MATTHEW 7:7 (NIV)

Question: Do you have a desire in your heart? Why not ask God for your heart's desires and watch what he does for you!

Memory Verse #31

But seek first the kingdom of God and his righteousness, and all these things will be added to you.

MATTHEW 6:33 (ESV)

Memory Verse #32

Don't be conformed to this world, but be transformed by the renewing of your mind, so that you may prove what is the good, well-pleasing, and perfect will of God.

ROMANS 12:2 (WEB)

Memory Verse #33

For the word of God is living and active, and sharper than any two-edged sword.

HEBREWS 4:12 (WEB)

FACT: The word of God is ALIVE! As you memorize scripture, watch it come to life in your heart.

Memory Verse #34

Let's therefore draw near with boldness to the throne of grace, that we may receive mercy and may find grace for help in time of need.

HEBREWS 4:16 (WEB)

 Did you know? God invites you to come near to his throne of grace, because he longs to be with you, and to help you.

Memory Verse #35

Jesus said to them, "I am the bread of life. Whoever comes to me will not be hungry, and whoever believes in me will never be thirsty.

JOHN 6:35 (WEB)

Memory Verse #36

I lift up my eyes to the mountains—
where does my help come from?
My help comes from the Lord,
the Maker of heaven and earth.

PSALM 121:1-2 (NIV)

Memory Verse #37

The joy of the LORD is your strength.

NEHEMIAH 8:10 (NLT)

Reminder: Any time you are sad, God's joy can be your strength. Lean on him the next time you're struggling or feeling down.

Memory Verse #38

The LORD doesn't see things the way you see them. People judge by outward appearance, but the LORD looks at the heart.

1 SAMUEL 16:7 (NLT)

Memory Verse #39

Worthy is the Lamb who was slain To receive power and riches and wisdom, And strength and honor and glory and blessing!

REVELATION 5:12 (NKJV)

Memory Verse #40

I have been crucified with Christ, and it is no longer I who live, but Christ lives in me.

GALATIANS 2:20 (WEB)

Memory Verse #41

So faith comes by hearing, and hearing by the word of God.

ROMANS 10:17 (WEB)

Memory Verse #42

For we are God's handiwork, created in Christ Jesus to do good works, which God prepared in advance for us to do.

EPHESIANS 2:10 (NIV)

Say this out loud today: I am God's handiwork, created to do good works.

Memory Verse #43

For it is God who works in you both to will and to work for his good pleasure.

PHILIPPIANS 2:13 (WEB)

Memory Verse #44

My God will supply every need of yours according to his riches in glory in Christ Jesus.

PHILIPPIANS 4:19 (WEB)

Say this out loud today: God WILL meet all my needs!

Memory Verse #45

Therefore, as you received Christ Jesus the Lord, so walk in him.

COLOSSIANS 2:6 (ESV)

Memory Verse #46

I just want to learn this from you: Did you receive the Spirit by the works of the law, or by hearing of faith?

GALATIANS 3:2 (WEB)

Remember: Without believing (faith) it is impossible to please God, and impossible to enter the Kingdom of heaven.

Memory Verse #47

Call to me and I will answer you, and will tell you great and hidden things that you have not known.

JEREMIAH 33:3 (ESV)

Memory Verse #48

And in him you too are being built together to become a dwelling in which God lives by his Spirit.

EPHESIANS 2:22 (NIV)

Memory Verse #49

Do not conform to the pattern of this world, but be transformed by the renewing of your mind. Then you will be able to test and approve what God's will is—his good, pleasing and perfect will.

ROMANS 12:2 (NIV)

Question:
What would it look like for you to live a life that doesn't conform to the world, but stands out for Jesus?

Memory Verse #50

BUT YOU, LORD, ARE A SHIELD AROUND ME, MY GLORY, AND THE ONE WHO LIFTS MY HEAD.

PSALM 3:3 (NASB)

Memory Verse #51

I SOUGHT THE LORD AND HE ANSWERED ME, AND RESCUED ME FROM ALL MY FEARS.

PSALM 34:4 (NASB)

Memory Verse #52

For in him we live, move, and have our being.

ACTS 17:28 (WEB)

Memory Verse #53

But Jesus said, "Let the children come to me. Don't stop them! For the Kingdom of Heaven belongs to those who are like these children."

MATTHEW 19:14 (NLT)

Reminder: Jesus loves being with you!

Memory Verse #54

He said to them, "Go into all the world and preach the Good News to the whole creation.

MARK 16:15 (WEB)

PS: This scripture is part of the 'Great Commission' where Jesus told his disciples and those who would one day follow Him (yes, YOU) to go out into all the world and tell others about him.

Memory Verse #55

In the beginning was the Word, and the Word was with God, and the Word was God.

JOHN 1:1 (WEB)

Memory Verse #56

So we fix our eyes not on what is seen, but on what is unseen, since what is seen is temporary, but what is unseen is eternal.

2 CORINTHIANS 4:18 (NIV)

Memory Verse #57

Where could I go from your Spirit? Or where could I flee from your presence?

PSALM 139:7 (WEB)

Reminder: There is nowhere in the whole wide universe you could run to, where God and his love could not find you.

Memory Verse #58

Seek the Lord while he may be found; call on him while he is near.

ISAIAH 55:6 (NIV)

Question: How can you seek God in your day-to-day life?

Memory Verse #59

Again he said, "Peace be with you. As the Father has sent me, so I am sending you."

JOHN 20:21 (NLT)

Memory Verse #60

I will say of the LORD, He is my refuge and my fortress: my God; in him will I trust.

PSALM 91:2 (KJV)

Memory Verse #61

He brought me to the banquet hall. His banner over me is love.

SONG OF SOLOMON 2:4 (WEB)

Memory Verse #62

The next day, he saw Jesus coming to him, and said, "Behold, the Lamb of God, who takes away the sin of the world!

JOHN 1:29 (WEB)

 Fun fact: In the Bible, 'The Lamb of God' is another name for Jesus, the one who died on the cross for YOU.

Memory Verse #63

And without faith it is impossible to please God, because anyone who comes to him must believe that he exists and that he rewards those who earnestly seek him.

HEBREWS 11:6 (NIV)

Memory Verse #64

I can do all things through Christ who strengthens me.

PHILIPPIANS 4:13 (WEB)

Memory Verse #65

One thing I ask from the Lord, this only do I seek: that I may dwell in the house of the Lord all the days of my life, to gaze on the beauty of the Lord and to seek him in his temple.

PSALM 27:4 (NIV)

What is one thing you would like to ask the Lord God today?

Memory Verse #66

Bring the whole tithe into the storehouse, that there may be food in my house. Test me in this," says the Lord Almighty, "and see if I will not throw open the floodgates of heaven and pour out so much blessing that there will not be room enough to store it.

MALACHI 3:10 (NIV)

Memory Verse #67

Then Jacob awoke from his sleep and said, "Surely the LORD is in this place, and I wasn't even aware of it!"

GENESIS 28:16 (NLT)

Memory Verse #68

For he raised us from the dead along with Christ and seated us with him in the heavenly realms because we are united with Christ Jesus.

EPHESIANS 2:6 (NLT)

Memory Verse #69

The disciples were amazed. "Who is this man?" they asked. "Even the winds and waves obey him!"

MATTHEW 8:27 (NLT)

These were the words spoken by the disciples after Jesus calmed a storm just by telling it to be still. If you were in the boat with them, what would you have said after seeing what Jesus did?

Memory Verse #70

Let your light so shine before men, that they may see your good works, and glorify your Father which is in heaven.

MATTHEW 5:16 (KJV)

Reminder: You are a light for Jesus in this world. Don't forget to let your light shine today.

Memory Verse #71

The LORD says to my Lord: "Sit at My right hand Until I make Your enemies a footstool for Your feet."

PSALM 110:1 (NASB)

Memory Verse #72

The steadfast love of the LORD never ceases; his mercies never come to an end; they are new every morning; great is your faithfulness.

LAMENTATIONS 3:22-23 (ESV)

Memory Verse #73

For truly, I say to you, if you have faith like a grain of mustard seed, you will say to this mountain, 'Move from here to there,' and it will move, and nothing will be impossible for you.

MATTHEW 17:20 (ESV)

 Did you know? It's not the size of your faith that matters, because even the smallest amount of faith is enough to see the impossible happen!

Memory Verse #74

EVERYONE THEN WHO HEARS THESE WORDS OF MINE AND DOES THEM WILL BE LIKE A WISE MAN WHO BUILT HIS HOUSE ON THE ROCK.

MATTHEW 7:24 (ESV)

PS: The "rock" that Jesus wants us to build our lives on is... HIM!

Memory Verse #75

BUT AS FOR ME, I KNOW THAT MY REDEEMER LIVES. IN THE END, HE WILL STAND UPON THE EARTH.

JOB 19:25 (WEB)

Memory Verse #76

For freedom Christ has set us free; stand firm therefore, and do not submit again to a yoke of slavery.

GALATIANS 5:1 (ESV)

Memory Verse #77

Finally, let the mighty strength of the Lord make you strong. Put on all the armor that God gives, so you can defend yourself against the devil's tricks.

EPHESIANS 6:10-11 (CEV)

Reminder: Don't forget to put on the armor of God today! To read more about the armor of God visit Ephesians 6:10-18 in your Bible.

Memory Verse #78

For He made Him who knew no sin to be sin for us, that we might become the righteousness of God in Him.

2 CORINTHIANS 5:21 (NKJV)

Say this out loud today: I am the righteousness of God in Christ Jesus.

Memory Verse #79

To them God chose to make known how great among the Gentiles are the riches of the glory of this mystery, which is Christ in you, the hope of glory.

COLOSSIANS 1:27 (ESV)

Memory Verse #80

Jesus then told the crowd and the disciples to come closer, and he said: If any of you want to be my followers, you must forget about yourself. You must take up your cross and follow me.

MARK 8:34 (CEV)

Memory Verse #81

Glory to God in highest heaven, and peace on earth to those with whom God is pleased.

LUKE 2:14 (NLT)

 This is what the angels sang in front of the shepherds on the night that Jesus was born. We often sing these words at Christmas time as we remember our savior's birth.

Memory Verse #82

For a child is born to us. A son is given to us; and the government will be on his shoulders. His name will be called Wonderful Counselor, Mighty God, Everlasting Father, Prince of Peace.

ISAIAH 9:6 (WEB)

 Did you know? This amazing verse was written nearly 600 years before Jesus' birth by the prophet Isaiah who was speaking about the birth of Jesus in the future.

Memory Verse #83

As therefore you received Christ Jesus the Lord, walk in him.

COLOSSIANS 2:6 (WEB)

Memory Verse #84

Seek the LORD and his strength; seek his presence continually!

1 CHRONICLES 16:11 (ESV)

Memory Verse #85

This is my command—be strong and courageous! Do not be afraid or discouraged. For the LORD your God is with you wherever you go.

JOSHUA 1:9 (NLT)

Reminder: God is with you today and every day. Don't be afraid because he is always near, even when you feel alone.

Memory Verse #86

Don't be afraid. I am with you. Don't tremble with fear. I am your God. I will make you strong, as I protect you with my arm and give you victories.

ISAIAH 41:10 (CEV)

Fun fact: There are over 100 scriptures in the Bible that tell us not to be afraid.

Memory Verse #87

But as for me and my house, we will serve the LORD.

JOSHUA 24:15 (NASB)

Memory Verse #88

But those who hope in the LORD will renew their strength. They will soar on wings like eagles; they will run and not grow weary, they will walk and not be faint.

ISAIAH 40:31 (NIV)

Memory Verse #89

*Trust in the Lord with all your heart,
And lean not on your own understanding;
In all your ways acknowledge Him,
And He shall direct your paths.*

PROVERBS 3:5-6 (NKJV)

Question: What can you trust God with today?

Memory Verse #90

The LORD is near to the brokenhearted And saves those who are crushed in spirit.

PSALM 34:18 (NASB)

 Remember: The next time you or someone you love is feeling broken-hearted, that is when God is close by, closer than the air you breathe.

Memory Verse #91

Don't get so angry that you sin. Don't go to bed angry.

EPHESIANS 4:26 (CEV)

Memory Verse #92

Those who are wise will shine as bright as the sky, and those who lead many to righteousness will shine like the stars forever.

DANIEL 12:3 (NLT)

Memory Verse #93

You will keep in perfect peace all who trust in you, all whose thoughts are fixed on you!

ISAIAH 26:3 (NLT)

Question: What does being in God's perfect peace mean to you?

Memory Verse #94

God's Kingdom doesn't come with observation; neither will they say, 'Look, here!' or, 'Look, there!' for behold, God's Kingdom is within you.

LUKE 17:20-21 (WEB)

Close your eyes and picture the Kingdom of God all around you. Jesus tells us that the Kingdom is everywhere, and it's also within us!

Memory Verse #95

For what shall it profit a man, if he shall gain the whole world, and lose his own soul?

MARK 8:36 (KJV)

Memory Verse #96

Set your mind on the things that are above, not on the things that are on the earth. For you died, and your life is hidden with Christ in God.

COLOSSIANS 3:2-3 (WEB)

Memory Verse #97

But thanks be to God, who in Christ always leads us in triumphal procession, and through us spreads the fragrance of the knowledge of him everywhere.

2 CORINTHIANS 2:14 (ESV)

Say this out loud today: I spread the fragrance of Jesus Christ wherever I go.

Memory Verse #98

I have told you these things, that in me you may have peace. In the world you have trouble; but cheer up! I have overcome the world."

JOHN 16:33 (WEB)

Memory Verse #99

I will put my laws into their mind; I will also write them on their heart. I will be their God, and they will be my people.

HEBREWS 8:10 (WEB)

Memory Verse #100

Work willingly at whatever you do, as though you were working for the Lord rather than for people.

COLOSSIANS 3:23 (NLT)

 Remember: Whenever you are working, doing chores, or even homework, do it all for God. Why? Because even the work we do can be like worship to him!

Salvation Prayer

If you want Jesus to be the Lord of your life, and spend eternity with him in heaven, the Bible says in Romans 10:9-10 that if you confess with your mouth and believe in your heart that Jesus is Lord, then you will be saved!

This is the most important prayer you could ever pray. If you are ready for Jesus to wash away your sins, live within your heart, and save your life for eternity, then why not grab a family member or friend, and pray this with them.

**Dear Jesus,
I am a sinner and I need you to save me.
I believe that you died on the cross, and your blood was shed for me.
Please forgive me of all my sins.
Come and live in my heart, and be the leader of my life, now and forever.
Help me to live for you, and be a shining light to others.**

Amen

Checklist

- [ ] John 3:16
- [ ] Romans 10:9
- [ ] 1 Peter 2:24
- [ ] 1 John 2:12
- [ ] Psalm 23:1-4
- [ ] John 13:35
- [ ] 1 Corinthians 13:1
- [ ] 1 Timothy 4:12
- [ ] 1 Corinthians 13:4-6
- [ ] Mark 12:30
- [ ] Psalm 119:105
- [ ] Psalm 91:1
- [ ] Psalm 91:11
- [ ] Jeremiah 29:11
- [ ] Philippians 4:6-7
- [ ] 1 Thessalonians 5:16-17
- [ ] Matthew 6:9-13
- [ ] 1 Peter 3:12
- [ ] Ephesians 6:1
- [ ] Proverbs 16:9
- [ ] Psalm 139:13-14
- [ ] Matthew 4:4
- [ ] Proverbs 9:10
- [ ] Hebrews 11:1
- [ ] Romans 8:28
- [ ] Matthew 6:20
- [ ] Proverbs 19:17
- [ ] Romans 8:31
- [ ] Matthew 6:25
- [ ] Matthew 7:7
- [ ] Matthew 6:33
- [ ] Romans 12:2
- [ ] Hebrews 4:12
- [ ] Hebrews 4:16
- [ ] John 6:35
- [ ] Psalm 121:1-2
- [ ] Nehemiah 8:10
- [ ] 1 Samuel 16:7
- [ ] Revelation 5:12
- [ ] Galatians 2:20
- [ ] Romans 10:17
- [ ] Ephesians 2:10
- [ ] Philippians 2:13
- [ ] Philippians 4:19
- [ ] Colossians 2:6
- [ ] Galatians 3:2
- [ ] Jeremiah 33:3
- [ ] Ephesians 2:22
- [ ] Romans 12:2
- [ ] Psalm 3:3

- ☐ Psalm 34:4
- ☐ Acts 17:28
- ☐ Matthew 19:14
- ☐ Mark 16:15
- ☐ John 1:1
- ☐ 2 Corinthians 4:18
- ☐ Psalm 139:7
- ☐ Isaiah 55:6
- ☐ John 20:21
- ☐ Psalm 91:2
- ☐ Song of Solomon 2:4
- ☐ John 1:29
- ☐ Hebrews 11:6
- ☐ Philippians 4:13
- ☐ Psalm 27:4
- ☐ Malachi 3:10
- ☐ Genesis 28:16
- ☐ Ephesians 2:6
- ☐ Matthew 8:27
- ☐ Matthew 5:16
- ☐ Psalm 110:1
- ☐ Lamentations 3:22-23
- ☐ Matthew 17:20
- ☐ Matthew 7:24
- ☐ Job 19:25
- ☐ Galatians 5:1
- ☐ Ephesians 6:10-11
- ☐ 2 Corinthians 5:21
- ☐ Colossians 1:27
- ☐ Mark 8:34
- ☐ Luke 2:14
- ☐ Isaiah 9:6
- ☐ Colossians 2:6
- ☐ 1 Chronicles 16:11
- ☐ Joshua 1:9
- ☐ Isaiah 41:10
- ☐ Joshua 24:15
- ☐ Isaiah 40:31
- ☐ Proverbs 3:5-6
- ☐ Psalm 34:18
- ☐ Ephesians 4:26
- ☐ Daniel 12:3
- ☐ Isaiah 26:3
- ☐ Luke 17:20-21
- ☐ Mark 8:36
- ☐ Colossians 3:2-3
- ☐ 2 Corinthians 2:14
- ☐ John 16:33
- ☐ Hebrews 8:10
- ☐ Colossians 3:23

CERTIFICATE

THIS CERTIFICATE IS PRESENTED TO

....

FOR MEMORIZING 100 BIBLE VERSES

_____
DATE

Did you enjoy this book? Consider leaving your feedback so others can enjoy it too!

We want to build an army of scripture warriors around the world! If you enjoyed this book, it would mean so much if you left a review so that other kids just like you can find it and start their scripture memorization journey.

www.ingramcontent.com/pod-product-compliance
Lightning Source LLC
Chambersburg PA
CBHW071250070526
44583CB00017B/2404